STAR WARS
THE
MANDALORIAN
THE ART & IMAGERY
COLLECTOR'S EDITION

VOLUME TWO

TITAN EDITORIAL
Editor Jonathan Wilkins
Managing Editor Martin Eden
Art Director Oz Browne
Senior Designer Andrew Leung
Assistant Editor Phoebe Hedges
Production Controller Caterina Falqui
Senior Production Controller
Jackie Flook
Sales and Circulation Manager
Steve Tothill
Marketing Manager Ricky Claydon
Direct Marketing Assistant
George Wickenden
Marketing and Advertisement
Assistant Lauren Noding

Publicist Imogen Harris
Editorial Director Duncan Baizley
Operations Director Leigh Baulch
Publishers Vivian Cheung &
Nick Landau

DISTRIBUTION
U.S. Newsstand: Total Publisher Services, Inc.
John Dziewiatkowski, 630-851-7683
U.S. Distribution: Ingrams Periodicals, Curtis
Circulation Company
U.K. Newsstand: Marketforce, 0203 787 9199
U.S./U.K. Direct Sales Market: Diamond Comic
Distributors
For more info on advertising contact
adinfo@titanemail.com

First edition January 2021

*Star Wars: The Mandalorian: The Art & Imagery
Collectors Edition: Volume Two* is published by
Titan Magazines, a division of Titan Publishing
Group Limited, 144 Southwark Street, London
SE1 0UP

Printed in the USA by Quad

For sale in the U.S., Canada,
U.K., and Eire

ISBN: 9781787735750
Titan Authorized User. TMN 14092

LUCASFILM EDITORIAL
Senior Editor Robert Simpson
Creative Director Michael Siglain
Art Director Troy Alders
Asset Management Bryce Pinkos,
Chris Argyropoulos, Erik Sanchez,
Gabrielle Levenson, Jason Schultz,
Nicole LaCoursiere, Sarah Williams
Story Group Leland Chee, Pablo Hidlago,
Matt Martin
Creative Art Manager Phil Szostak

Special Thanks: Tracy Cannobbio,
Christopher Troise, Shiho Tilley, Eugene
Paraszczuk, Dave Filoni and Jon Favreau

CONTENTS

THE
MANDALORIAN
& THE CHILD

" This is the way."

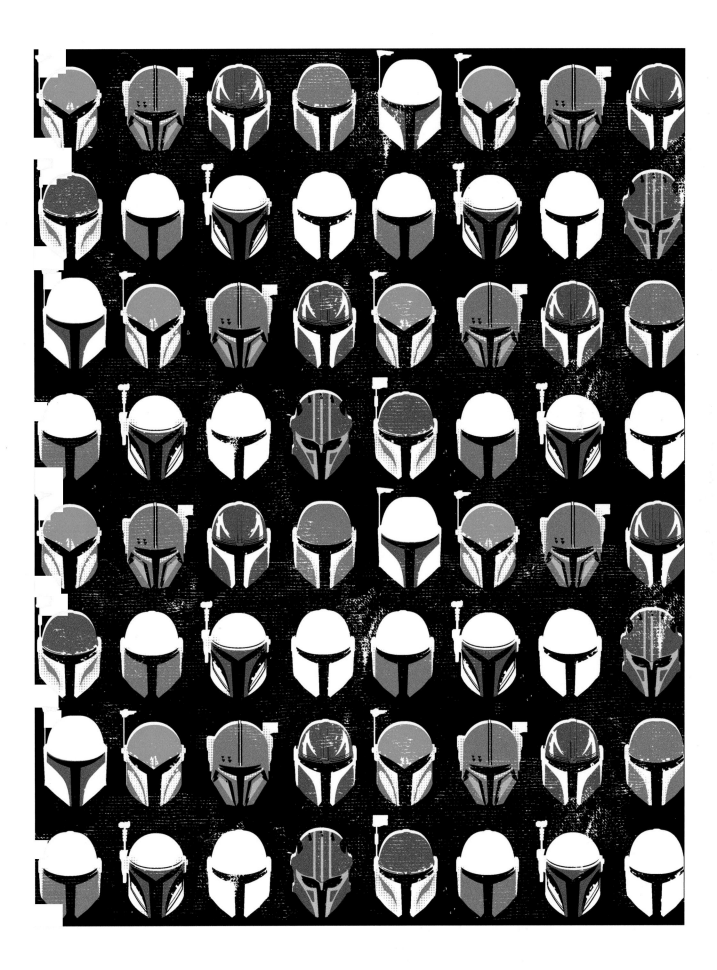

▲ ART BY **CHRISTIAN ALZMANN**

◀ ART BY
CHRISTIAN ALZMANN

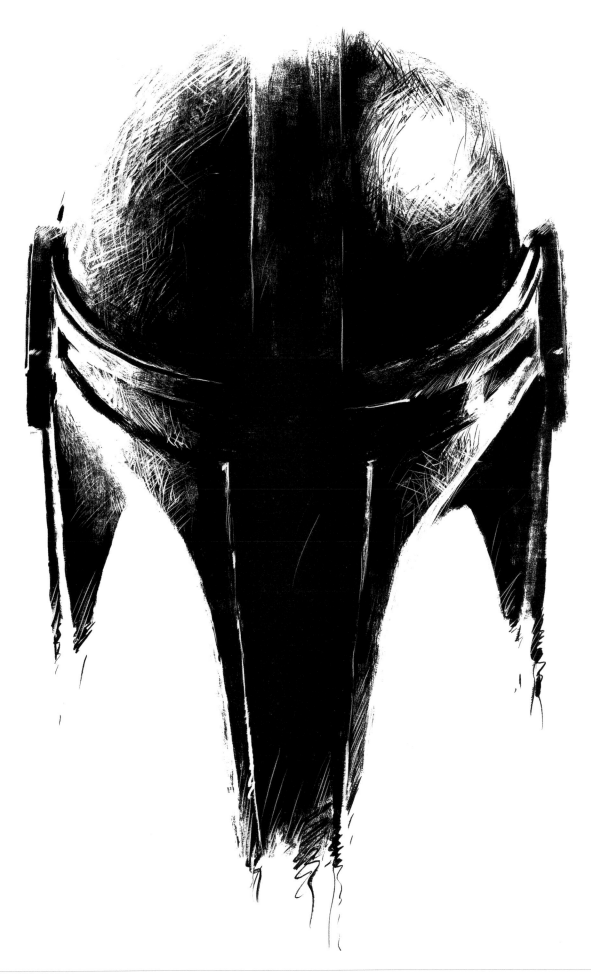

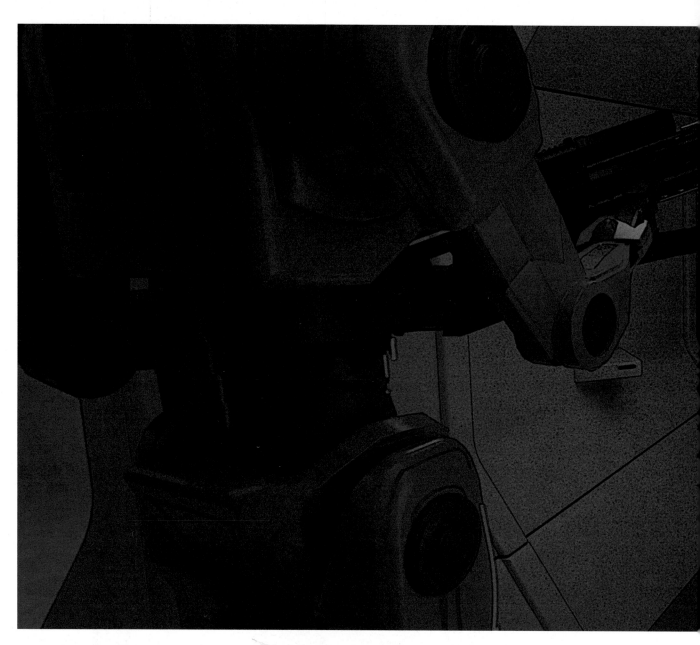

▲ ART BY **CHRISTIAN ALZMANN**

MANDO

BOUNTY HUNTER

12

▲ ART BY **BRIAN MATYAS**

▲ ART BY **BRIAN MATYAS**

LAWLESS
WORLDS

"Restore the
natural order."

▲ ART BY **ANTON GRANDERT**

▼ ART BY **CHRISTIAN ALZMANN**

▲ ART BY **RYAN CHURCH** ⦿

▲ ART BY **CHRISTIAN ALZMANN** ⦿

▲ ART BY **CHRISTIAN ALZMANN**

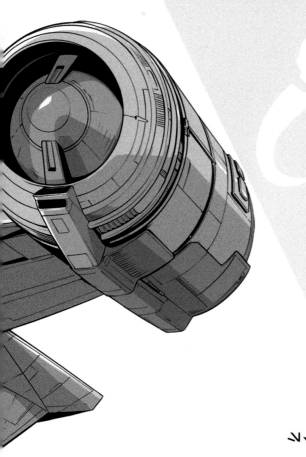

SECTION 5

STARSHIPS

"The best in the parsec."

▲ ART BY **CHRISTIAN ALZMANN**

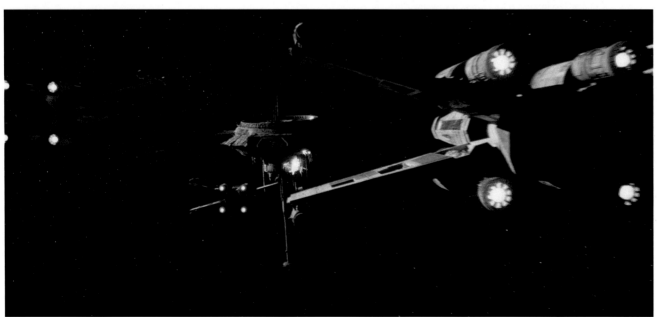

▲ ART BY **DAVID HOBBINS**

▲ ART BY **RYAN CHURCH**

▲ ART BY **RYAN CHURCH**

▲ ART BY **RYAN CHURCH**

▲ ART BY **CHRISTIAN ALZMANN**

Outlan
TIE

3/4 View

FIGHTER

ACTION FIGURES
SOLD SEPARATELY

Front

ENEMIES AND ALLIES

"Everybody play nice."

▲ ART BY **BRIAN MATYAS** 🐗

IG-11

(Eyegee-Eleven)

ACTION FIGURE

Front

Side

▲ ART BY **RYAN CHURCH**

JAWAS

▲ ART BY **CHRISTIAN ALZMANN**

ᖰᖰᑐᕀᖶᕒ

DROIDS

"Never trust
a droid."

▲ ART BY **CHRISTIAN ALZMANN**

CREATED ON THE GROUND

BATTLES ON THE GROUND

" Survival is strength. "

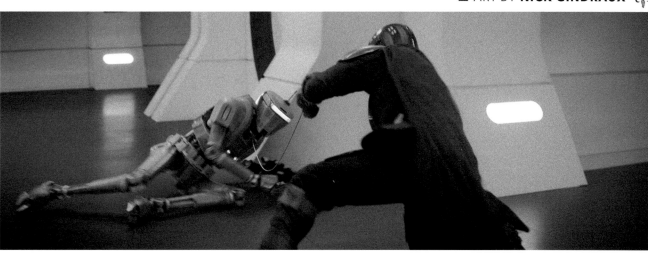

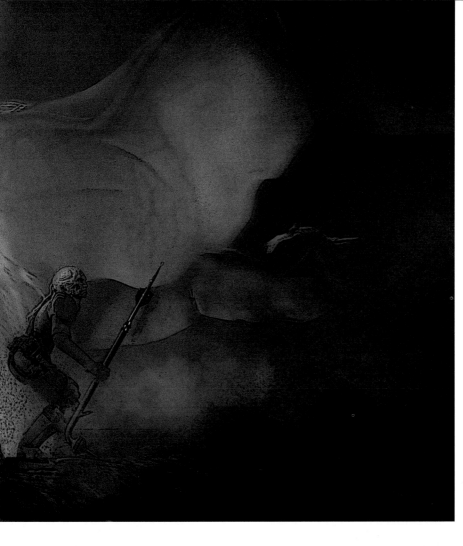

ART BY
CHRISTIAN ALZMANN

▲ ART BY **BRIAN MATYAS** ⟨⟩

▲ ART BY **NICK GINDRAUX** 🦅

▲ ART BY **BRIAN MATYAS, DOUG CHIANG,**

↓ΞVΙ ↓KↃV↓ ⚬Ɫ ↓ΞVΙ VΙⳞↃ17VΙ

THE LAST OF
THE EMPIRE

" Safety, prosperity,
opportunity, Empire. "

▼ ART BY **BRIAN MATYAS, DOUG CHIANG** 🏴

INCINERATOR

▲ ART BY **DOUG CHIANG, NICK GINDRAUX**

▼ ART BY
**ERIK TIEMENS,
DOUG CHIANG,
RYAN CHURCH**

MANDALORIAN STYLES

Tis the Season for the Bounty

Galaxy's Greetings

The MANDALORIAN

STAR WARS LIBRARY

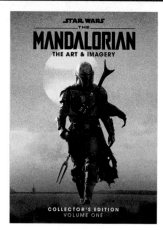

STAR WARS: THE EMPIRE STRIKES BACK: THE OFFICIAL COLLECTOR'S EDITION

THE MANDALORIAN THE ART AND IMAGERY VOLUME 1

STAR WARS: THE RISE OF SKYWALKER: THE OFFICIAL COLLECTOR'S EDITION

STAR WARS: THE SKYWALKER SAGA THE OFFICIAL MOVIE COMPANION

MARVEL LIBRARY

THE X-MEN AND THE AVENGERS GAMMA QUEST OMNIBUS

MARVEL STUDIOS' THE COMPLETE AVENGERS

MARVEL STUDIOS' BLACK WIDOW:

MARVEL: THE FIRST 80 YEARS

AVAILABLE AT ALL GOOD BOOKSTORES AND ONLINE

TITAN-COMICS.COM | **TITAN**BOOKS.COM